TOOLS FOR CAREGIVERS

- **F&P LEVEL:** B
- **WORD COUNT:** 25
- **CURRICULUM CONNECTIONS:** senses, sights, nature

Skills to Teach

- **HIGH-FREQUENCY WORDS:** a, I, my, see, with
- **CONTENT WORDS:** bug, clouds, eyes, flowers, kite, trees
- **PUNCTUATION:** exclamation point, periods
- **WORD STUDY:** long /e/, spelled ee (see, trees); /ow/, spelled ou (clouds); /ow/, spelled ow (flowers)
- **TEXT TYPE:** information report

Before Reading Activities

- Read the title and give a simple statement of the main idea.
- Have students "walk" through the book and talk about what they see in the pictures.
- Introduce new vocabulary by having students predict the first letter and locate the word in the text.
- Discuss any unfamiliar concepts that are in the text.

After Reading Activities

We see many things each day. The book showed us things we see outside. What else do you see outside? What does each thing look like? Do you use glasses to see them better like the girl on page 3? Have you ever used a magnifying glass to better see something small like the boy on page 6?

Tadpole Books are published by Jump!, 5357 Penn Avenue South, Minneapolis, MN 55419, www.jumplibrary.com

Copyright ©2023 Jump. International copyright reserved in all countries. No part of this book may be reproduced in any form without written permission from the publisher.

Editor: Jenna Gleisner   **Designer:** Emma Bersie

Photo Credits: Ilike/Shutterstock, cover; Andrew Makedonski/Shutterstock, 1; herjua/iStock, 2tl, 6–7; Thannaree Deepul/Shutterstock, 2tr, 12–13; Toey Toey/Shutterstock, 2ml, 4–5; Brandon Bourdages/Shutterstock, 2mr, 10–11, 16bl; Pakhnyushchy/Shutterstock, 2bl, 14–15, 16br; Artiste2d3d/Shutterstock, 2br, 8–9, 16tl; Amorn Suriyan/iStock, 3; karamysh/Shutterstock, 16tr.

Library of Congress Cataloging-in-Publication Data
Names: Nilsen, Genevieve, author.
Title: See / by Genevieve Nilsen.
Description: Minneapolis, MN: Jump!, Inc., (2023)
Series: My senses | Includes index.
Audience: Ages 3–6
Identifiers: LCCN 2022011520 (print)
LCCN 2022011521 (ebook)
ISBN 9798885240895 (hardcover)
ISBN 9798885240901 (paperback)
ISBN 9798885240918 (ebook)
Subjects: LCSH: Vision—Juvenile literature.
Classification: LCC QP475.7 .N43 2023 (print) | LCC QP475.7 (ebook) | DDC 612.8/4—dc23/eng/20220321
LC record available at https://lccn.loc.gov/2022011520
LC ebook record available at https://lccn.loc.gov/2022011521

MY SENSES
SEE

by Genevieve Nilsen

TABLE OF CONTENTS

Words to Know.............................2

See......................................3

Let's Review!...........................16

Index..................................16

WORDS TO KNOW

bug

clouds

eyes

flowers

kite

trees

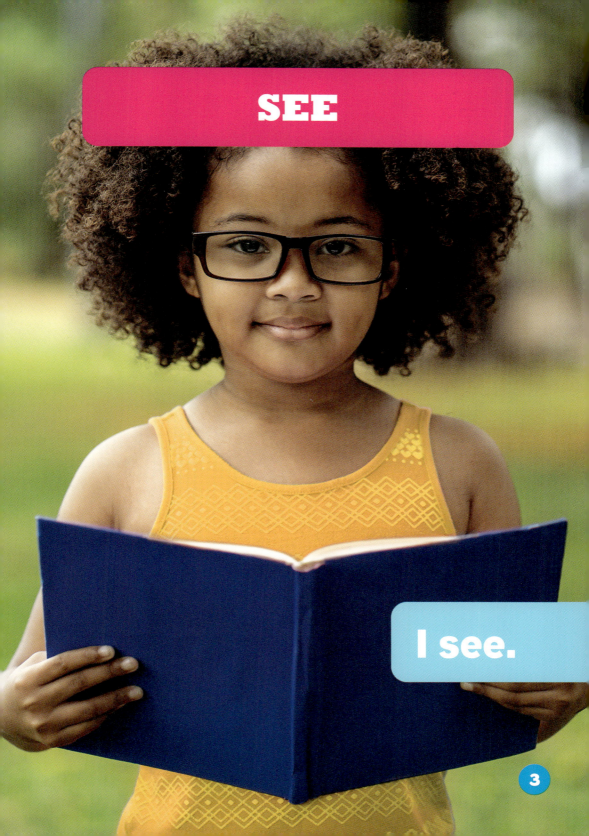

I see with my eyes.

I see a bug.

I see trees.

LET'S REVIEW!

We see with our eyes. Which of these pictures did you see in the book?

INDEX

bug 7
clouds 13
eyes 5
flowers 11

kite 15
see 3, 5, 7, 9, 11, 13, 15
trees 9